MAR 0 1 2013

I1031796

Wild SNOW

Skiing and Snowboarding

NEIL CHAMPION

A⁺
Smart Apple Media

Published by Smart Apple Media, an imprint of Black Rabbit Books
P.O. Box 3263, Mankato, Minnesota 56002
www.blackrabbitbooks.com

Printed in the United States of America at Corporate Graphics,
North Mankato, Minnesota

Library of Congress Cataloging-in-Publication Data
Champion, Neil.
 Wild snow : skiing and snowboarding / by Neil Champion.
     p. cm. -- (Adventure outdoors)
 Includes index.
 Summary: "Introduces readers to the snow sports of downhill skiing,
cross-country skiing, and snowboarding by presenting the basic
techniques, gear needed, and safety tips. Includes famous slopes
to visit, picture labels, and reading quiz"--Provided by publisher.
 ISBN 978-1-59920-808-4 (library binding)
 1. Skis and skiing--Juvenile literature. 2. Snowboarding--Juvenile
literature. I. Title.
 GV854.C512 2013
 796.93--dc23
                                2011051487

Created by Appleseed Editions, Ltd.
Designed and illustrated by Guy Callaby
Edited by Mary-Jane Wilkins
Picture research by Su Alexander

Picture credits
l = left, r = right, c = center, t = top, b = bottom

Page 1 Schalke Fotografie/Shutterstock; 2 Thinkstock; 4 Digital Vision/
Thinkstock; 5 Getty Images/Thinkstock; 6l Thinkstock, r Wikimedia
Commons/ Adrian8/Flickr; 7t Christophe Jossic/Shutterstock,
bl Morgan Lane Photography/Shutterstock, br Trekandshoot/
Shutterstock; 8t Thinkstock, b Eric Isselée/Shutterstock; 9l Thomas
Northcut/Thinkstock, c & r Stockbyte/Thinkstock; 10 Gorilla/
Shutterstock; 11l Demiter Petrov/Shutterstock, r Marcel Jancovic/
Shutterstock; 12 Karl Weatherly/Thinkstock; 14 & 15 Thinkstock;
16t Photos.com/Thinkstock, b Galyna Andrushko/Shutterstock;
17 Thinkstock; 18t Steve Estvanik/Shutterstock, b Maxx-Studio/
Shutterstock; 19, 20 & 21 Thinkstock; 22t Tan Wei Ming/
Shutterstock, c Titus Manea/Shutterstock, b Tomtsya/Shutterstock;
23l Elena Elisseeva/Shutterstock, r Daniel Wiedemann/Shutterstock;
24-25 Jupiterimages/Thinkstock; 25 Thinkstock; 26 Thinkstock;
27t Tyler Olson/Shutterstock, b Kaleb Timberlake/Shutterstock;
28t Steffen Foerster/Shutterstock, b Thinkstock; 29 Jupiterimages/
Thinkstock; 31 NotarYES/Shutterstock; 32t Andrey Armyagov/
Shutterstock, b Fedor Selivanov/Shutterstock:
Cover: Taavi Toomasson/Shutterstock

PO1443
2-2012

9 8 7 6 5 4 3 2 1

Contents

Let's Go Skiing!

You can enjoy snow sports on every one of the seven **continents** on earth. There are mountains and snowy places all around the world where you can ski or snowboard, experiencing the **adrenaline** rush of gliding across a magical landscape.

Amazing FACTS

People have used skis, sleds, and snowshoes for more than 20,000 years. Years ago, the world was much colder—snow and ice covered much more of the landscape than it does today. Cave drawings by the first early humans, known as Cro-Magnons, show them on skis. People were moving around on skis before wheels were invented.

Roald Amundsen was a Norwegian explorer. He was born in a land of snow and ice and was a very good skier. On December 14, 1911, he and four others became the first to reach the **South Pole**. They had been racing a British team led by Captain Robert Falcon Scott. Scott's team was nearly 310 miles (500 km) away and although they eventually reached the South Pole, they all died of cold, hunger, and exhaustion on the return journey. One reason Amundsen and his men survived was because they were much better skiers than the British men. They covered the 740 miles (1,190 km) across **Antarctica** much faster and used far less energy than the British.

Taking the Challenge

Before you start, you need to learn the skills that will keep you safe—not just skiing and snowboarding techniques—but also how to get fit, how to read a snowy landscape, and how to stay warm in cold conditions. You also need some first aid skills and need to know about the weather and how it can affect you in snowy places.

Getting Started

Snow sports can be expensive. You need to travel to places where there is enough snow and you need the right equipment. You may also need to buy a **lift pass** to ride up the slopes so you can ski or snowboard down again.

TRUE Survivors

Being disabled is no barrier to becoming a skier. Heath Calhoun was an airborne ranger in the US military in Iraq when his Humvee was hit during a rocket attack. His legs were so badly injured that they had to be amputated above the knee. Once he recovered, he decided to try skiing. Four years later, he became good enough at ski racing to take part in the 2010 Winter **Paralympics**.

Heath Calhoun carries the US flag at the Winter Paralympics.

Chairlifts carry people and their skis to the top of the slopes.

6

An artificial ski slope is a great place to practice snow sports.

Ski Clubs

Ski clubs offer information on the best **ski resorts** and the condition of the snow there. Snowfall varies from one year to the next. Ski clubs will also put you in touch with people who love the sport and can help you get started. You may be able to find cheap equipment and have some lessons through them.

Artificial Ski Slopes

A great way to spend time on the slopes without traveling hundreds of miles to the mountains is to use an artificial (or dry) ski slope. The earliest artificial slopes were made from bristly tiles and plastic brushes. Skis glided over them and could dig in when you wanted to turn. The materials used today look more like snow and give a better idea of what it is like to ski on snow.

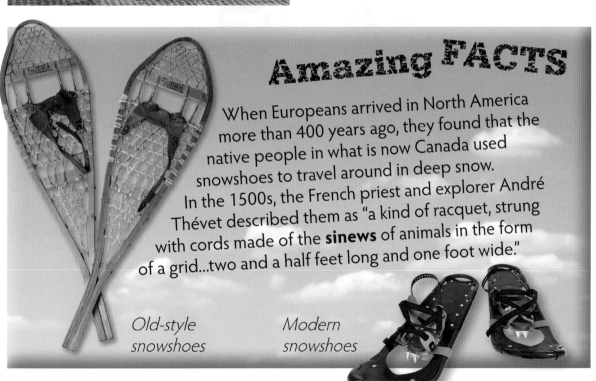

Amazing FACTS

When Europeans arrived in North America more than 400 years ago, they found that the native people in what is now Canada used snowshoes to travel around in deep snow.
In the 1500s, the French priest and explorer André Thévet described them as "a kind of racquet, strung with cords made of the **sinews** of animals in the form of a grid...two and a half feet long and one foot wide."

Old-style snowshoes

Modern snowshoes

Skiing Gear

hat

gloves

goggles

ski suit

ski poles

skis

ski boots

The right gear is essential if you are to get the most out of your time on the slopes, and you will need some expert advice on what to buy.

Clothing

Ski clothing should keep you warm when you are sitting on a ski lift or stuck in a **blizzard**. It also needs to allow your skin to breathe because you will get warm as you use your muscles gliding downhill or pushing across a flat landscape. The temperature high in the mountains is very cold, so you need a thin, warm layer against your skin —thermal tops and long johns are good **insulators**. Next put on a warm shirt and pants. For the outer layer, you need a windproof or padded ski suit or jacket and pants.

Amazing FACTS

The soft down feathers next to the skin of birds are perfect insulators. The feathers have a loose but strong structure that traps layers of air. Air holds heat well and keeps the birds very warm. The best down comes from geese and ducks and is used to make warm clothing and bedding.

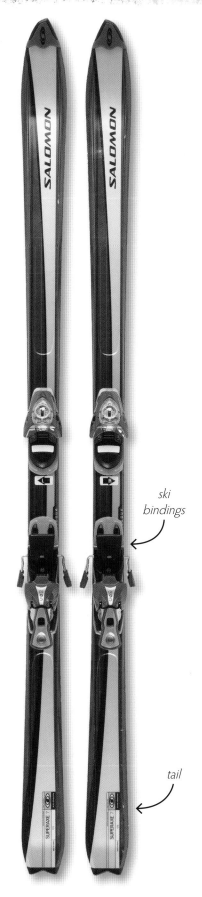

ski bindings

tail

TRUE Survivors

In February 2011, two men were skiing in Helen Lakes in Canada. They were about 7,875 feet (2,400 m) high and the temperature was frigid. One of the men caught his ski and twisted his ankle so badly that he could not stand on it. His friend skied off to find help, but it was more than three hours before a helicopter came to pick up the injured skier. He could not move during his wait, but he did have very good clothing, including a down jacket, and plenty of food and liquid. This meant that he did not get **hypothermia**, although he needed surgery to repair his ankle.

Choosing Skis and Boots

Skis have a turned-up front so they don't catch in the snow. They have a smooth, flat base so they slide easily. The edges are sharp and metallic to bite into the snow when you turn. The longer your skis, the faster you will go. To start with, do not wear skis taller than you are. Your ski boots must fit well—you need high, rigid boots for downhill skiing (to help when turning) and smaller, lighter boots for **cross-country skiing**.

Cross-country ski boots

Downhill ski boots

Snowboarding Gear

There are three main types of snowboards, and you need to understand the differences among them before choosing one. Snowboarders need similar clothing to skiers.

Types of Boards

A freestyle board is great for beginners. It is wide, stable, light, short, and flexible. This means you can move it around, turn easily, and use it for doing tricks.

Freeride boards are the most popular. They are good all-around performers, for both beginner and more experienced riders and can be used on both hard and icy or deep and powdery snow.

Freestyle

Freeride

Alpine

Goggles are especially useful when it is snowing.

The third type of board is an alpine. It is long, narrow, and stiff. It is good for carving out clean turns on wide slopes. Experienced boarders use this type of board.

Clothing

Like skiers, snowboarders wear a base layer, a mid layer, and an outer layer. The mid layer can be put on or taken off depending on temperature. The outer layer protects you from the wind and snow. Don't forget gloves and a hat (most boarders wear beanies). You will also need goggles and possibly a helmet. Boarders fall more than skiers, so parts of their clothing—knees, bottom, and backs—are reinforced for protection.

goggles

beanie hat

gloves

waterproof jacket

snowboarding pants

Amazing FACTS

Snowboarding began in the United States during the 1950s, but it took more than 30 years to become popular. Surfers took their skills to the snow slopes on custom-made boards. The first commercial boards were sold in the 1960s. An air of rebellion was linked to the sport and boarders were not allowed on ordinary ski slopes at first. Even in 1988, very few slopes allowed boarders. Ten years later the scene changed, and today most ski resorts welcome the youthful sport of snowboarding.

Young people enjoy the challenge of boarding tricks and stunts.

Getting Fit

Skiing and snowboarding are much more enjoyable if you are fit before you try them. There are plenty of exercises you can do at home and in open spaces near you to improve your fitness.

Working on Strength

Skiers need strong thigh (or quadriceps) muscles. These muscles work hard as you glide downhill with your knees bent, and they also power you on flat areas. Squat exercises help to strengthen these muscles.

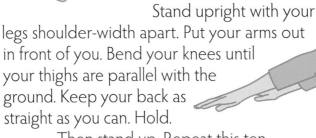

Stand upright with your legs shoulder-width apart. Put your arms out in front of you. Bend your knees until your thighs are parallel with the ground. Keep your back as straight as you can. Hold. Then stand up. Repeat this ten times, rest for one minute, then repeat again.

Two leg Squat

One leg squat

A harder version of this is the one leg squat. Balance on one leg with the other held out in front. Take your arms out in front of you and bend your knee. See how low you can go and then come up without falling over. Don't try to do too many at first—build up over time.

To do a split squat, you stand up and lunge one leg forward, keeping your thigh parallel with the ground. Lower your back knee as close to the ground as possible. Stay there for five seconds, then come up. Repeat ten times if you can.

Split squat lunge

Standing thigh stretch

Stretches

Stretching after exercising helps your body recover and prevents your muscles from being stiff the next day. There are several useful stretches for skiers, including the standing thigh stretch, the standing hamstring stretch, the groin stretch, and the hip stretch.

Standing hamstring stretch

Groin stretch

Hip stretch

Amazing FACTS

Your body responds to exercise by sending signals to the muscles you are using. Extra blood carrying energy-giving nutrients travels to the parts of the body that most need it. Other parts of the body are partly shut down. So when you exercise, less blood goes to your stomach and more goes to the muscles you are using. Your heart beats faster and your breathing rate increases so blood and oxygen move faster around your body. Eventually the muscles you are using will increase in size as they do more work and become more efficient.

Learning to Ski

Making your first slide downhill on a pair of skis can be scary. You need help from experienced people and one of the easiest ways to find this is to sign up at a ski school.

Learning to balance on one ski is harder than it looks.

Basic Technique

Once you put on skis, your feet will seem ten times larger than their normal size, and they don't grip the ground—they slide over it! You need to get used to skis on flat ground. Practice turning in a circle where you stand by moving the skis. Shift your weight from one foot to the other. Try lifting one ski in the air and balancing on the other, staying loose and relaxed. This is harder than you might think. Falling over a few times will help.

Amazing FACTS

Italian Simone Origone is the fastest man on skis. He traveled at 156.2 mph (251.4 kph) to set a world speed record in the French resort of Les Arcs in April 2006. Just one day later, at the same ski resort, Sanna Tidstrand from Norway set a new world record for the fastest woman on skis. She shot down the slopes at a maximum speed of 150.7 mph (242.59 kph).

The snowplow helps you turn and slow down.

Learn to Turn

You can graduate to a gentle slope to learn how to slow down and turn using the snowplow. Try to do this without using **ski poles**. Keep your skis parallel and aim down a gentle slope. As you gather speed, push out with your heels so the tail ends of your skis move out and the tips move together. The pressure you apply to your skis will make you slow down. If you press more on one side than the other, you start to turn.

TRUE Survivors

On April 23, 2007, American Barbara Hillary stood in one of the most hostile places on earth —the North Pole. She had skied there, braving **frostbite**, hunger, and polar bears. Many had done this in the past 100 years, but this woman was unique in several ways—she was 75 years old (one of the oldest to get there), she was the first black woman to reach the Pole, she had survived cancer, and she had not skied before this adventure. As she said, skiing "was not a popular sport in Harlem," where she grew up.

Learning to Snowboard

Snowboarding appeals to young people partly because boarders fall over much more than skiers do. You can also do more stunts and tricks on a snowboard once you have mastered the basics.

Snowboarders stand sideways to the slope when on their boards.

Body Position

Run forward in the snow and slide on your feet. The leading foot is the one you want in front on your snowboard. Buckle this one in first. On the board, distribute your weight evenly between your feet with your body and shoulders parallel to the board and head looking forward over your shoulder. To turn, shift your weight forward and lean on your toes or your heels, depending on which way you want to go.

Always strap your leading foot to the snowboard first.

Expect to fall over a lot when you are learning to snowboard.

Learning to Fall

Plenty of skiers and snowboarders are injured every year when they fall badly. The most common injuries are to knees, ankles, and wrists. Always try to fall to your toe-side, landing knees first in the snow, following with your hands clenched into a fist. This will help protect your wrists. Try to ride your board in a relaxed and flexible position, with knees bent and hands out.

TRUE Survivors

In March 2011, 24-year-old Nathan Scott was snowboarding in the Jasper National Park in the Canadian Rockies. He set off for one last big run before returning to the valley but became lost in a vast area of snow and rock. Without food, water, map, or compass, he needed help. After friends reported him missing, a rescue helicopter took nearly 24 hours to find him and return him unharmed to warmth and safety.

Thinking about Safety

Speeding downhill on a snowy slope is risky. When you are skiing, you need to match your level of skill with the challenge you take on.

Learning to ski at a ski school with an instructor is a great way to get started.

First things First

Start by going to a ski school to learn how to turn and stop on a **bunny hill**. Each level of difficulty requires greater skill and more experience. Make sure you don't take on too much before you are ready.

TRUE Survivors

In March 2011, two British skiers got lost in bad weather about 6,500 ft. (2,000 m) above an Italian ski resort. Charlotte Taylor and Matthew Kitchener strayed from the run into a dangerous **ravine**. They could not see in the blizzard and were **disoriented**. With no food, the sun setting, and the temperature falling, they were in trouble. At this point, they managed to call people in England, who alerted the Italian rescue team. The team took six hours to find them, and they were eventually taken to safety.

Hazards on the Slopes

Here are the main **hazards** to watch out for:

1 Other people
Collisions can be disastrous, so keep an eye on the other people around you.

2 Losing control
This can happen quite easily, especially when you are learning how to turn.

3 Dangerous areas
Avoid trees, fences, and cliffs. Some trees and fences have padding around them, and cliffs may have barriers to stop you from skiing over them.

DANGER
D'AVALANCHES

DANGER OF
AVALANCHES

LAWINEGEFAHR

5 Avalanches and whiteouts
In an avalanche, snow slides quickly down a slope and can carry you away and bury you. On slopes in ski resorts, avalanches are not usually a danger, but if you go **backcountry skiing**, you may get caught in one. A whiteout happens when it is snowing and you are in dense clouds. Everything looks white and there is no **horizon**. It is easy to get confused and end up lost.

4 Losing a ski
This may happen if you catch an edge or because your skis have not been tightened well enough to stay on your boots. Overtight connections are also a problem as they may prevent your skis from coming off when you fall. This can lead to a twisted knee, which is a common skiing injury.

Hitting the Slopes

Getting on to the slopes is what skiing and snowboarding are all about. Being on a snow-covered mountain and feeling the adrenaline rush of gliding downhill is an amazing sensation.

Weather and the Environment

Check the weather forecast for the day. Cloudy conditions can make it difficult to find your way, sunshine can overheat you, and wind can blow snow into your eyes, so wear goggles to protect them. Don't be surprised if you feel out of breath—your body will take time to adapt to the **altitude**. Many skiers take a small backpack with a little food and water as well as spare clothing and gloves.

TRUE Survivors

The highest point on earth is the summit of Mount Everest—29,035 ft. (8,850 m) high. In October 2000, Slovenian Davo Karnicar skied from the summit to base camp, a distance of 2.5 miles (4 km) and a vertical drop of around 11,483 ft. (3,500 m). The trek took him more than four hours.

A groomer prepares the snow for skiers and snowboarders.

The Slopes

In ski resorts, machines with tracks called groomers drive over the slopes to even out the snow. There are rope barriers near dangerous areas and trees and fences often have padding around them. You should carry a map of the area showing the ski runs.

Backcountry Skiing

Skiing backcountry means traveling over wild terrain. Trails are not prepared or evened, so the snow lies as it has fallen. The big risks of backcountry skiing are getting lost and being caught in an avalanche.

Ski Run Grades

Green Easy slopes; very broad and gently sloping

Blue Suitable for beginners but steeper than green runs; may be longer than green runs and go through more interesting areas

Red Suitable for intermediate skiers who can turn and stop easily; parts of red runs may be narrow or steep

Black The hardest runs at a resort—for expert skiers only; very steep in places

Where to Go

There are many ideal places for snow sports around the world. Europe and North America have the most resorts, but there are resorts in Australia, New Zealand, and South America with good snow.

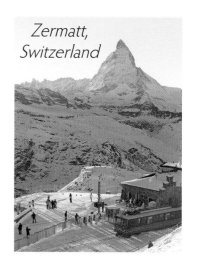
Zermatt, Switzerland

Lake Wanaka, New Zealand

Europe

There are ski resorts all over Europe, but the most famous resorts are scattered in the Alps mountains that cover parts of France, Switzerland, Italy, and Austria. The slopes can be crowded in February and March, which are the peak ski and snowboarding months.

St. Anton, Austria

North America

The resort of Snowbird-Alta in Utah has about 40 feet (12 m) of snow a year. Breckenridge in Colorado has easy, wide runs, which are great for beginners, and Jackson Hole in Wyoming has difficult runs for experts. Banff in Canada has a reputation as a good value resort for both skiing and snowboarding.

Banff, Canada

Amazing FACTS

Chacaltaya, Bolivia

❊ The world's highest ski resort is Chacaltaya in Bolivia, which is 17,785 feet (5,421 m) high.

❊ The world's longest ski run is the Vallee Blanche in France. It is 13.7 miles (22 km) long and drops almost 9,850 feet (3,000 m).

❊ One of the hardest ski runs in the world is the Swiss Wall in France. It is only 3,280 feet (1 km) long but drops 1,085 feet (331 m). A sign at the top warns: "For experts only."

Australia and New Zealand

The resort of Thredbo in Australia includes the country's highest peak, Mount Kosciusko—7,310 feet (2,228 m). Mount Baw Baw is another resort, three hours from Melbourne and a good place for beginners. The island of Tasmania has a ski resort called Ben Lomond.

New Zealand has mountains as high as 12,140 feet (3,700 m) in South Island and even a volcano that you can ski or snowboard down on North Island. The Lake Wanaka region has the largest area suitable for skiing. The season here runs from June to October.

Cross-country Skiing

Thousands of years ago, people used skis to travel over flat or gently sloping snow-covered ground rather than down steep mountains Today, cross-country skiing is still a popular activity.

TRUE Survivors

In January 2010, three cross-country skiers, Jesse, Christine, and Josiah, set off to cover part of a 9-mile (15 km) circuit of Mallard Creek in Yellowstone National Park. A series of incidents led to near disaster. They did not take the right equipment or enough emergency gear. Once on the trail, Josiah had problems with his skis and bindings. The snow was deep and their skis were too small to stay on the surface. Eventually, they took off their skis and walked, getting very cold feet. Exhaustion followed, and the three became separated as darkness fell. Fortunately, a rescue was organized when they failed to return before dark. Josiah had badly blistered and frostbitten feet, but all made a full recovery.

Away from the Crowds

While cross-country skiing, you can avoid crowded high mountain resorts and ski into the wilderness. You'll need a map and compass, as well as a backpack with an emergency kit. Norway has more than 400 cabins they call huts where cross-country skiers can stay, exploring large stretches of country on skis.

Different Equipment

Cross-country skis are much thinner and more flexible than downhill skis. Also, only the toe of your boot is clipped to a cross-country ski. This allows you to lift your heel, push off with your legs, and glide across flat country. Grooves on the bottom of the skis work to grip the snow as you push off to go forward.

Some skis have special waxes to help them grip, and you can also attach an extra layer called a skin to help you go uphill. Cross-country skiers use poles to help keep balance.

This cross-country skier enjoys the snowy hills.

Competitions

Skiers can compete in Alpine ski events, **Nordic (or cross-country) skiing, and ski jumping. The biggest events are held in the Winter Olympic Games which are held every four years.**

Alpine Events

These events include very exciting downhill racing, as well as slalom, giant slalom, and super giant slalom (or Super-G). Skiers race downhill one at a time over a specially prepared course. The fastest skier wins. The rules are simple, but the races are dangerous and crashes can be spectacular.

Slalom skiers weave between poles called gates set up on a course. If they pass a gate on the wrong side, they are disqualified. Competitors have two runs down the hill. The skier with the fastest time is the winner.

Slalom

Ski Jumping

Ski jumpers slide down a huge ramp on very large skis, taking off at the end of it. The aim is to glide through the air as far as possible, making the longest jump. Skiers are given points for distance but also for the quality of their glide and landing. The world record is held by Norwegian Johan Remen Evensen—in 2011 he jumped an incredible 808.7 feet (246.5 m).

Ski jump

Snowboarding Events

The International Snowboard Association sets the rules for all snowboarding competitions. The main snowboarding events in the Winter Olympics are:

Half-pipe

❄ **Half-pipe:** Boarders are awarded points for jumps and stunts as they ride down a u-shaped arena.

❄ **Parallel giant slalom:** Boarders ride down a prepared course and the boarder with the best time over two attempts wins.

❄ **Boardercross:** Four to six competitors ride together down a course full of bumps and banks of snow. The first past the post wins.

All three events have separate men's and women's competitions.

WINTER PARALYMPICS

There are snow sport competitions for disabled competitors all around the world today. The biggest event is the Winter Paralympic Games, held every four years, which began in 1976 in Sweden. Events include Alpine downhill races, slalom races, and cross-country skiing.

What do you know about snow sports?

Are you ready to take on the challenge of skiing or snowboarding down the slopes of a mountain resort or sliding cross-country into the wilderness? Do you know the difference between a blue run and a black run? Can you remember which is the highest ski resort in the world? Take this quiz to find out how much you know about the great snowy outdoors. Answers are on page 31.

1 Which of these statements is correct?

a A beginner's skis should be taller than they are.

b You should wear goggles or sunglasses to protect your eyes.

c The edges of your skis should be sharp so you can cut into the snow to turn.

d You should have rigid legs and stiff knees when snowboarding.

e You don't need to worry about avalanches when skiing backcountry.

2 The highest ski resort in the world is in which country?

a The US   **b** England   **c** France   **d** Bolivia

3 Snowboarding began in the US in the 1950s. True or false?

DANGER D'AVALANCHES

DANGER OF AVALANCHES

LAWINEGEFAHR

4 A snowplow is:

a Turning the tips of your skis inward and pushing out with your heels to slow down and make a gentle turn

b Another name for a snowboard

c A type of bird that lives high on snowy mountains and plows through the snow with its beak looking for food

d A place where you can stop to get food and refreshments

5 Which ski slopes are suitable for a beginner?

a Black runs   **b** Green runs   **c** Blue runs   **d** Red runs

6 Half-pipe is a snowboarding term that describes:
a A broken pipe
b A large U-shaped arena where snowboarders do tricks and stunts
c A place where you can relax and hang out with other snowboarders
d A type of chairlift for snowboarders

7 What does altitude mean?
a The height of something (a mountain summit or ski resort) above sea level
b Somebody's manner and way of speaking to other people
c Getting really cold in the high mountain air
d A term used by one snowboarder for another

8 People have been skiing for more than 20,000 years.
True or false?

9 Cross-country skis are much thinner than Alpine or downhill skis.
True or false?

10 Name the stretch

Glossary

adrenaline A chemical made in our bodies to help us run fast from danger or fight it.

altitude The height of something above sea level.

Antarctica The southern-most continent on earth; At its center is the South Pole.

backcountry skiing To ski off marked trails; You need to be very experienced to try backcountry skiing.

blizzard A combination of strong wind and snow; It is very difficult to see in a blizzard.

bunny hill Very gentle slope used by ski instructors to teach beginners the basic skills of skiing or snowboarding.

continent One of the seven huge land masses on earth—Asia, Africa, North America, South America, Antarctica, Europe, and Australia.

cross-country skiing A style of skiing that involves traveling across flat landscapes with gentle hills rather than down mountains.

disoriented Being lost and not knowing which way to go.

frostbite Damage to skin caused by extreme cold.

hazard Something that can harm us; On a ski slope, hazards might include trees, fences, or rocks skiers could collide with—or avalanches.

horizon The line in the distance where the sky meets the ground.

hypothermia A very dangerous condition in which someone becomes so cold that they lose consciousness and may die.

insulator Warm, inner layer that keeps out the cold.

lift pass A ticket you buy to travel up a mountain on ski lifts and ski chairs.

Nordic A style of skiing that started in Norway rather than the Alps; Cross-country skiing is a type of Nordic skiing.

Paralympics The Olympic games for people with disabilities.

ravine A large gouge in the side of a mountain, often carved out by a river.

sinew Another word for tendon—the tough fiber in our bodies that attaches muscle to bone.

skin Strips of material that stick to the bottom of a ski that allow it to slide forward but also grip the snow when pushing off; Cross-country skiers use skins to ski uphill.

ski poles Poles skiers hold to help keep their balance.

ski resorts Specially built villages in the mountains with hotels, restaurants, ski lifts, and runs for skiers.

South Pole The most southern point on earth at the center of Antarctica.

Websites

www.fis-ski.com The International Ski Federation
www.skiclub.co.uk The Great Britain Ski Club
www.ussa.org The US Ski and Snowboard Association
www.disabledskiing.ca A Canadian website for disabled skiers
www.snow.co.nz The New Zealand Snow Sports Council

Books

Alpine and Freestyle Skiing (Winter Olympic Sports) Kylie Burns, Crabtree Publishing, 2010
Skiing (Extreme) Heather C. Hudak, ed., Weigl Publishers, 2009
Winter Sports (QEB Get Active!) Barbara Bourassa, QEB Publishing, 2007

Quiz Answers

1 *b and c*

2 *d*

3 *True*

4 *a*

5 *b and c*

6 *b*

7 *a*

8 *True*

9 *True*

10
a Standing thigh stretch
b Standing hamstring stretch
c Groin stretch
d Hip stretch

Index